# FLY GUY PRESENTS: SNAKES

## Tedd Arnold

Scholastic Inc.

For Judy and Gary, who have many
snake stories to tell!—T. A.

Thank you, Sara Ruane, for your contributions to this book.

Photo Credits:
Photos ©: cover: Biosphoto/Superstock, Inc.; 2–3 background: Rob Hainer/Shutterstock, Inc.; 4 top left: Vibelmages/iStockphoto; 4 top right: Chaitud Pongthanaiporn/Dreamstime; 4 center: Danun13/Dreamstime; 4 bottom: Greg Dale/National Geographic Creative; 5: Stefan Schierle/Fotolia; 6 main: Dr. Tim Davenport/WCS; 6 inset: luther2k/Fotolia; 7 left: bitis73/iStockphoto; 7 right: John Cancalosi/Ardea; 8 top left: Courtesy of Sara Ruane; 8 top center left: Dennis Donohue/Dreamstime; 8 top center right: Shannon Plummer/Thinkstock; 8 top right: sky-navin/iStockphoto; 8 center top: Courtesy of Sara Ruane; 8 center bottom left: the4js/iStockphoto; 8 center bottom right: Courtesy of Sara Ruane; 8 bottom: FrankRamspott/iStockphoto; 9 top left: Twildlife/Dreamstime; 9 top right: Kitto Studio/Shutterstock, Inc.; 9 bottom: Paul Sutherland/National Geographic Creative; 10: Mgkuijpers /Dreamstime; 11: Design Pics/Thinkstock; 12: pitchwayz/iStockphoto; 13 top left: Rujitop/iStockphoto; 13 top right: benzinefoto/iStockphoto; 13 bottom: Lightwriter1949/iStockphoto; 14 top: Paul & Joyce/Animals Animals; 14 bottom: Kevin & Suzette Hanley/Animals Animals; 15 top left: alptraum/iStockphoto; 15 top right: ZiZ7StockPhotos/Shutterstock, Inc.; 15 bottom: Narcis Parfenti/Shutterstock, Inc.; 16 top: Pat Canova/Alamy Images; 16 bottom: MR1805/iStockphoto; 17 top: Ingo Arndt/Minden Pictures/National Geographic Creative; 17 bottom: Nicolas Perrault III/Wikimedia; 18 top: Duncan Usher/Ardea; 18 bottom: Animals Animals/Superstock, Inc.; 19 left: Michael Fogden/Animals Animals; 19 right: Mc Donald Wildlife Photog./Animals Animals; 20 top: Mark Kostich/Thinkstock; 20 bottom: Andrew Bee/Getty Images; 21 top: reptiles4all/Shutterstock, Inc.; 21 bottom left: LittleStocker/Shutterstock, Inc.; 21 bottom right: mark higgins/Shutterstock, Inc.; 22: Zigmund Leszczynski/Animals Animals; 23 top: Paul Freed/Animals Animals; 23 bottom: ER Degginger/Science Source; 24: Pete Oxford/Getty Images; 25: David M. Dennis/Animals Animals; 26 top: mariaflaya/iStockphoto; 26 bottom: Byronsdad/iStockphoto; 27 top: EcoPrint/Shutterstock, Inc.; 27 center: Mary Clay/Ardea; 27 bottom: Tim Laman/National Geographic Creative; 28 left: Courtesy of Sara Ruane; 28 right: Joe Riis/National Geographic Creative; 29 top left: Don Arnold/Getty Images; 29 top right: Steven David Miller/Animals Animals; 29 bottom: Gregory G. Dimijian, M.D./Science Source.

The publisher does not have any control over and does not assume any responsibility for author or third-party websites or their content.

ISBN 978-0-545-85188-6

Copyright © 2016 by Tedd Arnold.

12 11 10 9 8 7 6 5 4 3 2 1            16 17 18 19 20

Printed in the U.S.A.            40
First printing, January 2016
Designed by Rocco Melillo

A boy had a pet fly named Fly Guy.
Fly Guy could say the boy's name —

"I know where to find snakes at the zoo," said Buzz. "Look! It's the Snake House!"

Fly Guy was curious.

"Snakes aren't as scary as people think," said Buzz. "Let's find out more!"

They opened the door and stepped inside . . .

Snakes are reptiles. Lizards, turtles, and crocodiles are reptiles, too.

HORNED LIZARD

CROCODILE

TURTLE

All reptiles have scaly skin, lungs for breathing, and backbones.

• SNAKE SKELETON •

Reptiles are ecototherms (ek-toe-therms). They cannot create their own body heat. They need sunlight to warm their bodies.

RED-TAILED RATSNAKE

It looks like this snake is having fun in the sun!

Scales protect a snake's body and help it move. Scales are made of keratin—the same material as human fingernails!

Some snakes' scales grip the ground like tire treads. Then muscles help them slither forward.

As a snake grows, it sheds its skin. It sheds all of its scales—even those covering its eyes! The new skin underneath looks bright and shiny.

CORN SNAKE SHEDDING

BOA CONSTRICTOR SHEDDING

Many snakes use the color and texture of their scaly skin to make it harder for other animals to see them. This is called camouflage (KAM-uh-flahzh).

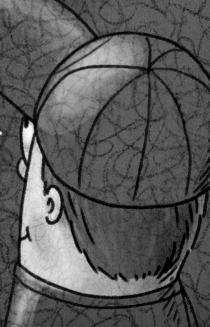

BUZZ?

There are more than 3,000 kinds of snakes in the world.

Cope's vine snake

mangrove snake

tree python

cobra

bushmaster

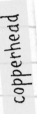

copperhead

long-nosed snake

Snakes live on every continent except Antarctica.

NORTH AMERICA
SOUTH AMERICA
EUROPE
ASIA
AFRICA
AUSTRALIA
ANTARCTICA

the seven continents

Most snakes live on land. Snakes can live almost anywhere — in grasslands, wetlands, deserts, forests, swamps, trees, and caves. Some snakes even live in the ocean!

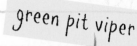
green pit viper

diamondback rattlesnake

All snakes can swim, but sea snakes have flat tails. These special tails make it easier for them to move through water.

olive sea snake

check out its flat tail!

Humans have five senses — sight, hearing, taste, smell, and touch. Snake senses are similar, but snakes sometimes use different body parts for these functions.

Snakes have two eyes but no eyelids. Most snakes can only see what is right in front of them, and it is often blurry. A clear scale called a brille (BRILL-a) covers each eye for protection.

Snakes never close their eyes!

Snakes do not have external ears. They do not hear sounds the same way as humans. They feel sounds as vibrations (vi-BRAY-shuns) in their bodies.

NO EARZZ!

AFRICAN BUSH VIPER

Snakes use their nostrils to breathe, not to smell. They have forked tongues that help them taste AND smell.

Snakes flick out their tongues to pick up chemicals in the air. The taste of these chemicals tells them food is nearby.

NORTHERN BLACK-TAILED RATTLESNAKE

Snakes' scales allow them to feel the texture of things they slither over, like sand, dirt, grass, or water.

BURMESE PYTHON

KING COBRA

NORTH AMERICAN WATER SNAKE

Some snakes have a sixth sense.

Pit vipers have special organs called pits between each eye and nostril. These pits allow the snake to see the body heat of animals nearby. That means pit vipers—such as rattlesnakes—can hunt in the dark!

Mojave rattlesnake

**HUNTZ FLYZZ?**

black-tailed rattlesnake

snake "pit"

Pythons and boas also have pits. Their pits are located on the lips and lower jaw. These snakes sense the heat of nearby animals.

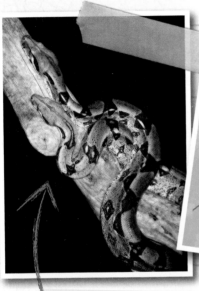

boa constrictors

albino Burmese python

snake "pit"

green tree python

Snakes have lived on Earth for about 140 million years.

The largest snake ever discovered was the Titanoboa. It weighed around 2,500 pounds.

● TITANOBOA WAS MORE THAN 40 FEET LONG ●

Titanoboa lived around 58 million years ago. That's 5 million years after T. rex roamed the earth, but this prehistoric giant was just as scary!

● T. REX

The largest snake alive today is the green anaconda. Most anacondas grow as long as a pickup truck. Some can be even longer!

GREEN ANACONDA

The smallest snake is the Barbados threadsnake. It is less than four inches long.

CUTE-ZIE!

BARBADOS THREADSNAKE

Snakes eat and kill other animals, called prey (PRAY). Snakes can eat small mammals, birds, fish, worms, and even other reptiles or snakes.

DICE SNAKE

Some snakes, like boas and pythons, are constrictors. They coil their bodies around their prey and squeeze until the animal stops breathing.

BOA CONSTRICTOR SQUEEZING PREY

The bottom of a snake's jaw is loosely attached to the snake's skull rather than to the top jaw. This allows a snake to open its mouth wide enough to swallow the animal whole.

BALL PYTHON

COMMON EGG-EATING SNAKE

Could a snake swallow me?!

Many snakes, like cobras, mambas, vipers, and rattlesnakes, bite their prey. The snake's sharp fangs shoot a deadly poison called venom (VEN-uhm) into the animal's body.

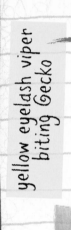

yellow eyelash viper biting Gecko

The poison weakens, paralyzes, or kills the animal. Then the snake swallows it whole.

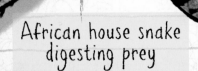

African house snake digesting prey

Great Lakes bush viper

FLYZZ BITEZ TOO!

Sometimes snakes bite humans. Many snake bites can be treated with a special medicine called antivenom (AN-tee-ven-uhm). Antivenom helps the body defend itself from the poison.

scientists use snake venom to create antivenom

About three-quarters of the world's snakes lay soft, leathery eggs. These snakes are oviparous (oh-VIP-er-uhs).

EASTERN HOGNOSE SNAKES

BABYZZ!

Fly Guy, they may not like milk.

Most snakes lay their eggs somewhere warm, like in a hole in the ground, under a log, or in a nest of leaves. Then the snake leaves the eggs to hatch on their own.

But other snakes—like the python and the king cobra—stick around to warm or protect their eggs.

ANGOLAN PYTHON

Not all snakes lay eggs. Viviparous (vie-VIP-er-uhs) snakes give birth to live babies. Anacondas, many sea snakes, and most vipers are viviparous.

NEWBORN COPPERHEADS WITH MOTHER

Rattlesnakes have special hard pieces on their tails. These hard pieces are made of keratin, the same material as snake scales. When a rattlesnake shakes its tail, these pieces vibrate and create a rattling sound. This sound warns predators to stay back.

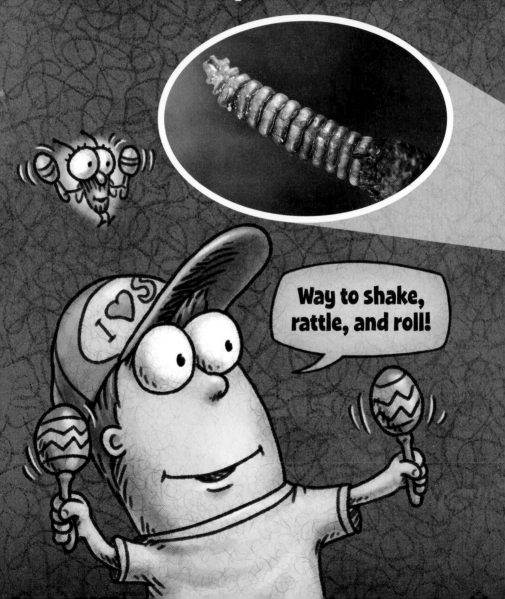

Way to shake, rattle, and roll!

Every time a rattlesnake sheds its skin, it grows another piece on its tail. But don't try to guess a rattlesnake's age by counting its rattles! Snakes can shed a few times a year, and rattle pieces can break off easily.

MIDGET FADED
RATTLESNAKE

Some snakes live just a few years in the wild. Others can live to be more than 25

People believe many things about snakes. Some of these things are true, but some are false.

1. A snake can grab its tail in its mouth and roll after prey. **FALSE!** A stressed snake may bite its own tail by mistake. But "hoop snakes" are not real.

2. Snakes can hypnotize people. **FALSE!** They look like they are staring because they don't have eyelids.

3. Snakes dance to music. **FALSE!** A snake might look like it's dancing because it can sometimes follow the movements of a flute.

4. Snakes hiss. **TRUE!** Some snakes can push air through an organ in their throats. This makes a hissing sound.

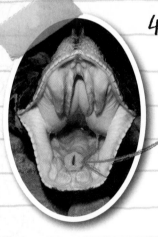

5. Flying snakes are real. **TRUE!** (sort of) Some tree-climbing snakes can push off into the air and glide down to the ground.

A scientist who studies snakes is called a herpetologist (hur-puh-TAH-luh-jist).

HERPETOLOGIST HOLDING A PIT VIPER

HERPETOLOGIST HOLDING A BLUNT-HEADED TREE SNAKE

Some herpetologists study toxic snake venom and hope to use it to create cures for human diseases. Someday, venom that makes it hard for animals to stop bleeding could help save someone who is having a heart attack!

Other herpetologists work at zoos or museums. They teach people about snakes and other reptiles.

BOA CONSTRICTOR

DUMERIL'S BOA

We sure learned a lot!

"Wow!" said Buzz. "I had no idea just how cool snakes really are!"

Buzz and Fly Guy could not wait for their next field trip.